MARVEL

WHAT WOULD SPIDER-MAN DO?

A STUDIO PRESS BOOK

First published in the UK in 2021 by Studio Press,
an imprint of Bonnier Books UK Limited,
4th Floor, Victoria House, Bloomsbury Square, London, WC1B 4DA
Owned by Bonnier Books,
Sveavägen 56, Stockholm, Sweden

www.bonnierbooks.co.uk

© 2021 MARVEL

1 3 5 7 9 10 8 6 4 2

All rights reserved

ISBN 978 1 80078 031 6

Written by Susie Rae
Edited by Sophie Blackman and Saaleh Patel
Designed by Rob Ward
Production by Emma Kidd

The views in this book are the copyright holder's own and the copyright,
trademarks and names are that of their respective owners and are not intended
to suggest endorsement, agreement, affiliation or otherwise of any kind.

A CIP catalogue for this book is available from the British Library

Printed and bound in Italy

BULLIES...

WHEN SOMEONE TRIES TO
START TROUBLE IN THE HALLWAY,
IT'S IMPORTANT TO TAKE
THE HIGH GROUND.

I TAKE A DEEP BREATH, SMILE
AND WALK ON BY LIKE I HAVEN'T
EVEN NOTICED THEY ARE THERE...

... NO MATTER HOW TEMPTING IT
MIGHT BE TO WEB THEM TO A WALL.

LOSING YOUR KEYS...

WITH A JOB THAT INVOLVES SWINGING ALL OVER THE NEIGHBOURHOOD, BUSTING CRIME AND HELPING THE PUBLIC, I SEEM TO CONSTANTLY LOSE MY KEYS MID-SWING.

TO BE SAFE, I NOW LIKE TO HIDE A SPARE SET OF KEYS SOMEWHERE IN THE CITY, OR MAYBE TWO SETS...

... OR THREE, OR FOUR, OR FIVE. I LOSE A LOT OF KEYS.

ASKING SOMEONE ON A DATE...

I'VE GOT TO BE HONEST, THIS REALLY ISN'T MY STRONG SUIT.

THE LAST TIME I TRIED TO ASK SOMEONE OUT, I MANAGED TO WALK INTO TWO DIFFERENT DOORS AND GET MY NAME WRONG. SHE SEEMED TO THINK IT WAS CUTE, THOUGH, SO MAYBE IT WORKED.

OKAY, YES, THIS MIGHT SOUND LIKE A WEIRD AND SPECIFIC SITUATION THAT OTHER PEOPLE WILL NEVER FIND THEMSELVES IN, BUT IT'S MORE COMMON THAN I FIRST THOUGHT.

ANYONE WHO ENDS UP GETTING BITTEN BY ONE OF THOSE GLOWY LITTLE CRITTERS HAS A SURPRISINGLY HIGH CHANCE OF GETTING SOME SUPER-COOL POWERS.

BUT, HONESTLY, THEY SHOULD PROBABLY GET IT CHECKED OUT BY A DOCTOR...

WORK-LIFE BALANCE...

LIFE CAN GET BUSY, PARTICULARLY WHEN JUGGLING SCHOOL, WORK, HOBBIES AND A PART-TIME GIG SAVING THE NEIGHBOURHOOD FROM CRIMINALS. IT'S HARD TO CATCH A BREATHER, SOMETIMES.

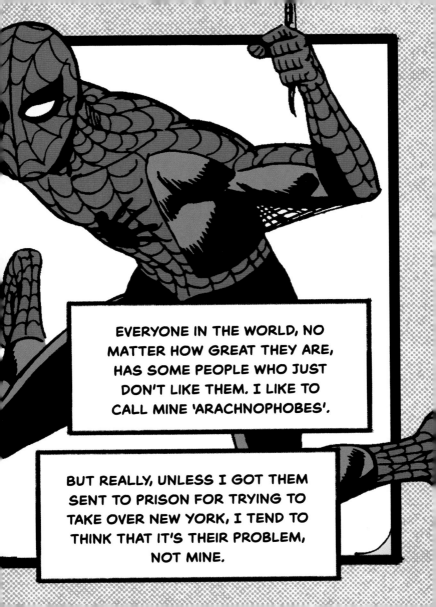

NOBODY'S GOOD AT ABSOLUTELY EVERYTHING, NOT EVEN IRON MAN (ALTHOUGH, TO BE FAIR, HE IS GOOD AT A LOT OF THINGS).

INSTEAD OF WORRYING ABOUT THE THINGS WE'RE BAD AT, WE SHOULD FOCUS ON THE THINGS WE'RE GOOD AT. FOR EXAMPLE, I MIGHT NOT BE GOOD AT KNOWING WHEN TO STOP TALKING...

... BUT I'M GREAT AT SCALING BUILDINGS, WISECRACKING AND TRIPPING OVER STUFF.

RUNNING LATE...

I'LL BE HONEST, HERE. ON THE OCCASIONS WHERE I CAN'T SHAVE OFF A FEW MINUTES FROM MY TRAVEL TIME BY *THWIPPING* ACROSS THE ROOFTOPS, I TEND TO BE LATE.

LUCKILY, IN THIS DAY AND AGE, IF I CALL AHEAD AND SAY THAT MY TRAIN HAS BEEN WAYLAID BY A SUPER VILLAIN ATTACK, PEOPLE USUALLY ACCEPT IT. THEY'RE SO COMMON, NOBODY EVER CHECKS.

WITNESSING A CRIME...

I ENCOURAGE MY SPIDEY FANS NOT TO COPY ME IF THEY WITNESS A CRIME...

... UNLESS THEY HAVE SUPER STRENGTH, SUPERHUMAN HEALING ABILITIES, A STYLISH SPIDER-SUIT AND A FULL BOTTLE OF WEB-FLUID.

OTHERWISE, THEIR MAIN PRIORITY SHOULD BE GETTING THEMSELVES TO SAFETY WHILE TRYING NOT TO STUMBLE ACROSS ANY VATS OF CHEMICALS OR STRANGE LASERS ON THEIR WAY OUT.

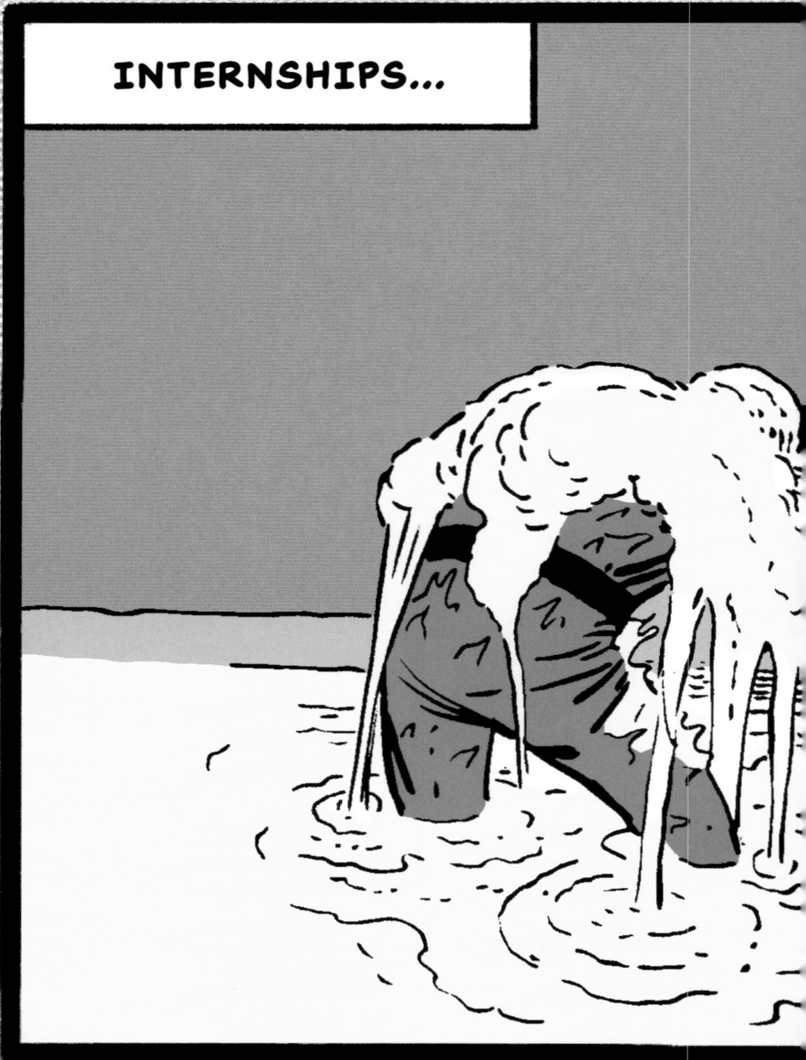
INTERNSHIPS...

IN MOST SITUATIONS, HONESTY IS THE BEST POLICY. 'BUT, SPIDEY,' I HEAR PEOPLE SAY, 'DON'T YOU HAVE A WHOLE SECRET IDENTITY THAT NOBODY KNOWS ABOUT?'

WELL, YES. BUT I GOT BITTEN BY A RADIOACTIVE SPIDER AND HAVE TO PROTECT A WHOLE NEIGHBOURHOOD FROM CRIME EVERY DAY, SO I'M ALLOWED TO TELL A COUPLE OF LITTLE WHITE LIES.

STAYING ACTIVE...

THERE'S ALMOST NOTHING BETTER THAN GETTING OUTDOORS AND MOVING AROUND.

FOR PEOPLE LIKE ME, WHO LIVE IN A TINY, INNER-CITY APARTMENT, IT'S EVEN MORE IMPORTANT TO GET OUTSIDE, OTHERWISE WE START TO GO A LITTLE CRAZY.

GO FOR A WALK! SCALE A BUILDING! PARKOUR ACROSS SOME ROOFTOPS!

TAKING PUBLIC TRANSPORT...

PUBLIC TRANSPORT IS GREAT! IT'S CHEAP, IT REMOVES THE NEED TO FIND PARKING AND THERE ARE ALL SORTS OF INTERESTING CHARACTERS TO BUMP INTO. I'VE TAKEN SOME WILD RIDES IN MY TIME...

... ON TOP OF TRAINS, WEBBED TO THE BACK OF MOVING BUSES, SAVING FERRIES FROM LOOMING DANGER.

BUT HONESTLY, JUST GETTING A TICKET, SITTING DOWN AND LISTENING TO A PODCAST OR SOMETHING IS WAY LESS STRESSFUL.

FOLLOWING YOUR DREAMS...
MY UNCLE BEN USED TO TELL ME, ALWAYS FOLLOW YOUR DREAMS!
UNLESS THEY'RE SUPER-WEIRD DREAMS ABOUT ACCIDENTALLY GETTING SENT INTO SPACE OR BEING CHASED BY A MAN DRESSED LIKE A GIANT VULTURE...
... DON'T FOLLOW THOSE DREAMS.

EVEN FOR PEOPLE WHOSE SIBLINGS AREN'T QUITE AS... UNIQUE AS THE AVENGERS, IT'S STILL BEST TO BE NICE TO THEM AS MUCH AS POSSIBLE.

ESPECIALLY WHEN THOSE SIBLINGS HAVE THE ABILITY TO LIFT AN ENTIRE CAR WITH ONE HAND.

MAKING NEW FRIENDS...

I USED TO FIND MAKING FRIENDS HARD, BUT IT TURNS OUT IT'S WAY EASIER WHEN WE HAVE STUFF IN COMMON. NOWADAYS, I HAVE FRIENDS WHO LOVE SCIENCE, JUST LIKE ME...

... AND SEVERAL OTHERS WHO ALSO HAVE RADIOACTIVE SPIDER BITE-RELATED POWERS THAT THEY USE TO FIGHT CRIME.

GETTING COFFEE...

WHEN GETTING COFFEE TO GO,
I ALWAYS BRING MY OWN CUP
FROM HOME. THIS IS BETTER
FOR THE ENVIRONMENT, YES...

... BUT ALSO, MY CUP HAS A
PROPER LID. PERFECT FOR
DRINKING COFFEE UPSIDE DOWN.

DID I WANT TO BATTLE INVADING ALIENS? PROTECT THE WORLD FROM HYDRA? TRAVEL TO DIFFERENT MULTIVERSES AND SEE WHAT'S GOING ON THERE?

IN THE END, WE HAVE TO PICK THE THING THAT FEELS RIGHT. ME? I'LL TAKE BEING A FRIENDLY NEIGHBOURHOOD SPIDER-MAN OVER TRAVERSING THE GALAXY ANY DAY. SPACE IS SCARY.

SPOTTING A SPIDER IN YOUR HOUSE...

PEOPLE SHOULD BE NICER TO SPIDERS, MAN! THEY'RE PROBABLY MINDING THEIR OWN BUSINESS...

... AND ONLY REALLY BOTHER PEOPLE WHO START TRYING TO TAKE OVER THE CITY OR SOMETHING.

WORKPLACE SAFETY...

I LIKE TO GO THROUGH A CHECKLIST BEFORE I SET OFF ON ANY NEIGHBOURHOOD-PROTECTING ADVENTURES. MAKE SURE I HAVE ENOUGH WEB-FLUID — TICK.

KEEP MY MASK SECURELY FASTENED SO IT DOESN'T SLIP OFF AT AN INCONVENIENT MOMENT — TICK. STICK TO BUILT-UP AREAS WHERE IT'S POSSIBLE TO *THWIP* AWAY TO SAFETY IF NEEDED — TICK.

THIS ADVICE IS RELEVANT FOR MOST JOBS, PROBABLY.

... I EVEN MET A GIRL WITH SQUIRREL POWERS. I LIKE TO THINK THEY WERE INSPIRED BY YOURS TRULY, WHICH JUST GOES TO SHOW...

... ROCKING A LOOK THAT WORKED FOR ME WAS WAY BETTER THAN FOLLOWING AN EXISTING TREND.

OTHER MARVEL BOOKS...